ABOUT THE AUTHOR

Meet Mishica Moon, the beloved primary school teacher and children's author from London. As a child, she loved books and storytelling, which led her to pursue a career in education. Mishica's unique teaching methods and love for her students inspired her to write children's books that reflect their diverse experiences and contain important messages. She believes all stories have something to teach us. When she's not writing or teaching, Mishica advocates for education and literacy. Her books transport readers to magical lands and remind them of the magic in the world. Anything is possible with the imagination!

Thank you to all the amazing
children I've taught

Text and images by Mishica Moon

First published 2024

The rights of Mishica Moon are to
be identified as the author of this work.

All rights reserved. No part of this publication may be reproduced, stored in a retrieval system or reproduced or transmitted in any form or by any means, electronic, mechanical, photocopying, recording or otherwise, without prior consent.

Introduction

Hey there, grown-ups!

Welcome to... Positive Power:
25 Tips to Boost Your Child's Confidence.

You're in the right place if you've ever worried about your child feeling shy or unsure. Confidence isn't something kids are just born with; it's something grownups can help them build, bit by bit, day by day.

Think about all the amazing things your child can do when they believe in themselves. They can make new friends, try out for the school play or speak up in class. It's a fact that confidence opens so many doors. And most of all… you get to be their guide on this adventure!

This book is packed with free, easy tips you can use immediately. No fancy words, no complicated steps—just honest, poetic advice that works.

Whether your child is naturally confident or a bit on the shy side, these tips will help them feel strong and ready to take on the world with a smile.

Welcome to "25 Tips to Boost Your Child's Confidence." Follow these rhythmic tips to help your child shine like a star every day of the week!

Happy reading and happy boosting!

Tip 1:

Be Yourself

You're so unique, so shine, shine, shine,

Show the world you're truly divine.

In a wonderful world where dreams aspire,

Embrace your quirks and release your fire.

For in being true to who you are,

Golden light will light your star.

So stand tall and show the world you're proud,

In your uniqueness, confidence is loud.

You are special, so see it through,

Just be yourself and remain true.

Tip 2:

Practice Makes Perfect

Keep practising what comes from the heart,
It doesn't have to be perfect–just start.
In everything that you pursue,
Practise with passion; it's your due.
With every try, you'll learn and grow,
Improve each day 'til talent shows.
Don't let things get in your way;
Following your heart, you'll see better days.
Soon, you'll see your dreams manifest,
And soon, you'll see that you're the best.

Tip 3:

Speak Up

Open your mouth. Let your voice out.
Speaking up shows you have no doubt.
In every moment, talk loud and clear;
Sharing thoughts will wipe out fear.
Don't hide your light; don't pout.
Soon, you will really learn to shout.
Be brave and release words to the sky,
For in these words, inner strength lies.

Tip 4:

Try New Things

Explore new things and give them a go.

New ideas put you in the flow.

In our beautiful world, there's much to see,

Being creative makes you feel wild and free.

Why don't you reach for the sky?

Why not aim and jump up high?

With each new step, you will find,

Growth and learning one day at a time.

Tip 5:

Set Small Goals

Set small goals you can achieve.
Each success makes you believe.
In life's journey, take it slow;
Smart goals make your confidence grow.
With each step forward, you will see,
Success builds up, creating a new me.
So aim for the stars, but start with what's near;
Make your vision water-clear.
In reaching your goals, you'll start to see
More miracles than you could ever believe.

Tip 6:

Be Positive

Stay optimistic when things go wrong.
Positivity makes you strong.
When skies are dark and days seem long,
Positive minds can't go too far wrong.
Though storms may rage like a tempest,
Positivity meets you at your best.
Look for the light when things aren't too bright;
Keep your spirits high while you fight the fight.

Tip 7:

Learn from Mistakes

Mistakes help you to learn and grow.
They make you wiser, this we know.
In every trip, in every fall,
Mistakes teach morals, big and small.
They're stepping stones along the way,
Pushing you forward, come what may.
Don't be afraid to make a fabulous mistake,
As from them, greater progress you'll make.
With each setback, you'll surely find
Mistakes help to expand your mind.

Tip 8:

Help Others

Helping others makes you feel divine,
A feeling that will make you shine.
By lending a hand and sharing a smile,
This makes others feel life's worthwhile.
It's not just good for them, but you who gain
Pure wonder, like a double rainbow after rain.
So be a light for others, stand by their side,
Use your kindness to help and guide.
For in lifting people, you'll surely find
Helping others makes you truly kind.

Tip 9:

Stay Active

Play and exercise each day.
Staying active keeps worries away.
Play every day, like monkeys in trees.
In games and fun, your worries will cease.
Staying active, come what may,
You won't notice the time of day.
For in play and exercise, you'll surely find
Staying active brings peace of mind.

Tip 10:

Keep Learning

Learning new things expands your mind.
Knowledge makes you search and find.
With books in hand, let curiosity explore;
Learning new things opens doors.
On every page, a world to mine,
Expanding your mind, a thought at a time.
For in learning new things, you'll surely find
Knowledge opens those portals in your mind.

Tip II:

Be Prepared

Being prepared helps you feel sure.
Confidence comes when you're secure.
With plans in place, you're ready for opportunity.
Being prepared opens up many possibilities.
So prepare yourself; stand tall and strong.
In being ready, you can't go wrong.
For in feeling prepared, you'll surely find
Confidence and success bring peace of mind.

Tip 12:

Stay Organised

Keep your space tidy and clean,
Organised spaces keep your mind keen.
In every corner, every nook,
Keep the space tidy, like a rule book.
With clutter cleared and order found,
Your mind stays sharp, your thoughts unbound.
For in keeping things clean, you'll surely find
An organised space keeps you aligned.

Tip 13:

Believe in Yourself

Believe in yourself, and you have the power.
Confidence looms like a tall tower.
In your heart lies your brute strength;
Believe in yourself. Go to any length.
With every step, your power grows,
Confidence blossoms, and it will show.
Leave doubts well in the past,
Gain strength in abilities that last.
For in believing in yourself, you'll surely find
Confidence blossoms like a rose in your life.

Tip 14:

Take Breaks

Taking breaks is good for your soul.
It refreshes your mind and keeps you whole.
When life feels heavy along the way,
Taking breaks lightens your day.
In moments of rest, your spirit revives,
Ready to tackle, ready to strive.
So pause, breathe, let worries fade;
In rest and play, peace is made.
For in taking breaks, you'll surely find
Peace is recharged in body and mind.

Tip 15:

Find Your Talents

Discover what you love to do.
Your talents are unique to you.
In passions found, your heart will soar;
Life will open talent doors.
In every hobby, every pursuit,
Your skills will bear the ripest fruit.
So dig deep and let your talents bloom;
Life's centre stage will make you room.
For in discovering what makes you tick,
Your talents will rise oh so quick.

Tip 16:

Be Kind to Yourself

Be kind to yourself; don't be tough.
Love yourself, know you're enough.
In the mirror's reflection, be gentle and kind,
Be loving to you in heart and mind.
In every scar, find beauty and grace,
Embrace yourself and love your face.
So be gentle, be kind, let self-love shine,
In loving yourself, find peace, be divine.
For in being kind to yourself, you'll find
Loving you is enough in heart and mind.

Tip 17:

Surround Yourself with Positivity

Stay close to those who make you smile.
Treasure the relationship 'cause it's worthwhile.
True friendships make your world so bright;
Positive energies merge with light.
Cherish the bonds that you appreciate;
Loyal friendships reciprocate.
For staying close to friends, you'll find
Love lasting forever in your heart and mind.

Tip 18:

Stay Curious

In every adventure is something to explore;
Learning makes you grow more and more.
So let your mind wander, and let your spirit roam;
In exploration, new seeds are sown.
For down curiosity's avenue, you'll surely find
Discoveries are healthy for your mind.

Tip 19:

Stay Calm

Stay calm when things don't go your way.
Inner calm brings peace that will stay.
When thunder cracks and skies turn grey,
Breathe deeply and let worries drift away.
So breathe in, breathe out, and remember to pray;
In calmness, find strength, come what may.
For in staying calm, you'll surely find
You're untouchable when you have a calm mind.

Tip 20:

Ask Questions

Don't be afraid to ask. It's smart.

Questions reveal the boldest heart.

In every moment, don't you wait;

If you need an answer, don't hesitate.

So get straight to the point, let your voice ring clear;

In asking, creates courage without fear.

For in asking questions, you'll surely find

They show confidence in thought and mind.

Tip 21:

Be Grateful

Gratitude fills you with good cheer.
It shows the universe that you care.
In every dawn, in every night,
Gratitude shines like a guiding light.
In counting blessings, your heart will soar,
You'll receive good tidings forevermore.
For in gratitude's embrace, you'll surely find
Love and peace in heart and mind.

Tip 22:

Stand Tall

Stand tall and walk with pride.
Courage will stay by your side.
With every step, hold your head high;
Let your confidence amplify.
So let all your doubts fall away;
Stand tall and approach each new day.

Tip 23:

Celebrate Yourself

Celebrate your wins, no matter the size;
Every success is a worthy prize.
In victories, grand or victories small,
Embrace them each, one and all.
In every triumph, your spirit burns bright;
Celebrating yourself puts you in the light.
So cheer and let it all out;
Celebrating wins gives something to shout.
Every success counts, big or small;
Don't forget one and all!

Tip 24:

Dream Big

Dream big dreams and aim so high.

Possibilities are endless if you only try.

You must aim to reach the sky;

Dream big dreams. Let your spirit fly!

Set your sights on ambition that soars;

In chasing dreams, you'll find satisfaction and more.

For in aiming high, you'll surely find

Dreams come true in heart and mind.

Tip 25:

Keep Smiling

A smile can light the darkest room.
A smile can make another bloom.
A smile shines a ray of pure light.
A smile can be so wide and bright.
For in sharing your smile, you'll surely find
Like attracts like; it's all in the mind.

Conclusion

Thanks for joining us on this journey!

You've made it through Positive Power: 25 Tips to Boost Your Child's Confidence.

We hope you found some useful titbits. Remember, building confidence isn't about making big changes; it's about the little moments every day where you show your child they're loved, amazing, and capable of achieving anything their little hearts desire.

Keep encouraging your child to try new things, be the number one cheerleader as they succeed, and have a comfort cushion when things don't go to plan. This alone will help their confidence to grow because they'll soon realise that no matter what happens, they have the support of someone who believes in them. Remember, no parent manual exists, and you're doing a great job. You make a huge difference every time you help your child confidently step into their future.

Here's to many more confident, happy moments ahead!

All the best,

Mishica Moon

Thank you for reading Positive Power: 25 Tips to Boost Your Child's Confidence.

Readers mean a lot to me because your support encourages me to write more.

If you enjoyed Positive Power: 25 Tips to Boost Your Child's Confidence, please leave a review on Goodreads.

It will help other readers take a chance on this book or others.

Happy reading, and thank you again for being part of the Mishica Moon adventure!

Check out mishicamoonbooks – https://www.mishicamoonbooks.com

www.ingramcontent.com/pod-product-compliance
Lightning Source LLC
Chambersburg PA
CBHW081412070526
44583CB00020B/2776